GAIA

Detox the
Spring clean your organs
natural way

HEALTH ALL YEAR ROUND

Treating your body to an "inner spring clean" guarantees vitality and wellbeing. Delicious foods bring new vigour, give a stimulus to the metabolism, put the liver, gallbladder, and kidneys into tiptop working order, purify the blood, and rid the body of excess fluid. The traditional time for a detox is in the spring—the Christian practice of fasting for Lent is a typical example. Then especially, in the weeks leading up to Easter, there is an abundance of foods ideal for the purpose. Some of these are in fact available all year round, so that a "detox" is possible whatever the season.

A SLUGGISH SYSTEM

Nature normally takes care of the "ins" and "outs" of the food we eat. If the "outs" part of the process is no longer functioning as well as it might, it is possible for unwanted by-products and waste substances to accumulate in the body. They are deposited in the blood vessels, joints, tissues, organs, and muscles. In the long term, serious illnesses can result. The first indications that inner cleansing is not functioning as well as it might are constant fatigue and lack of concentration, listlessness, chronic headache, and susceptibility to infections. Skin impurities, frequent digestive upsets, and muscle and joint pains can also signal the need for a "detox". These are warning signals given by your body. Do take them seriously. Treat your body to a general overhaul. This calls for nothing more dramatic than carefully thought out menus, conscious enjoyment of the foods themselves, sufficient exercise in the open air, long enough periods of relaxation, and a little pampering with skin and body care. You will emerge from it feeling newborn.

ORGANS RESPONSIBLE FOR DETOXIFICATION

LIVER: The liver can be described as the body's own chemical factory. It has the key role in enabling the body to use the food we eat. A great variety of chemical transformation processes happen there; the liver is where certain substances are broken down, and others are formed. As an organ, it is essential in the process of detoxification. We absorb more and more harmful substances—examples like smoking, alcohol, drugs, car exhaust fumes, chemicals, and heavy metals are familiar to us all. The task of putting things right falls on the liver. It also manufactures bile, which is particularly ⸱ortant for the digestion of fats.

KIDNEYS: The blood flows through the kidneys many times a day. The kidneys filter out any nutritionally useful substances, which are returned to the circulation, and any substances that are present in excess, or are actually harmful. These are removed from the body, excreted in urine made by the kidneys. The frequent, uncontrolled taking of medication, excess alcohol, and cystitis can, in the long term, damage the kidneys. They diminish in size and eventually cease functioning.

INTESTINES: A healthy intestinal flora acts on the food in the gut, taking out any nutritionally useful substances that have not yet been digested, and leaving the useless ones to be excreted. The greatest enemies of gut flora are antibiotics and food with too little roughage in it. Both hinder the smooth functioning of the digestive processes, damage the intestinal flora, and enable metabolic breakdown products to accumulate.

LUNGS: The role of the lungs in detoxifying the body mainly involves breathing out carbon dioxide, filtering out toxic substances from the air we breathe, and removing toxins present in the blood. Heavy smokers face an increased risk.

SKIN: A healthy skin protects the body against unwanted invaders. Sweating also rids the body of harmful substances through the skin.

Fitness
Enjoy that healthy feeling
each and every day

DAILY SELF-HELP GEMS

❋ Drink plenty. This is important to flush out the kidneys and carry away metabolic breakdown products.

❋ Keep active. Healthy exercise means breathing in plenty of oxygen, and the more you do this, the better your metabolism will be.

❋ Take time to eat, and chew slowly. The digestion of carbohydrates begins in the mouth.

❋Eat a low-fat diet. Fat is the last nutrient to be digested from the food, and it is a slow process. The liver will be taken up with its share of the task for a long time, leaving little spare capacity for its detoxification role. Result: the liver has almost no time to "recover".

❋ Avoid alcohol, tobacco, and medicines as far as is reasonable. Metabolizing these, too, makes great demands on your body's detoxification organs.

❋ Treat commercially ready-prepared meals as a last resort. They often contain many additives, such as flavourings and flavour enhancers, spelling hard work for the liver.

CHOICE OF FOOD MATTERS

❋ Eat plenty of carbohydrates, especially fibre-rich foods. The roughage promotes the activity of the intestines, and it is harder for unwanted substances to accumulate.

❋ Choose your food to provide a good intake of vitamins and minerals each day. These are both important to health, and fulfil a great many functions, enabling all the processes of the body to take place efficiently. They therefore ensure thorough removal of waste substances. Some are essential components of digestive juices.

❋ Eat raw fruit and vegetables as often as you can. Cooking destroys important ingredients in these foods. Raw foods also contain quantities of certain digestive enzymes which are beneficial. They belong to the class of foods rich in alkalis, which means they have a positive effect on the uric acid level.

❋ Give preference to alkali-forming foods such as raw fruit, vegetables, and salad leaves. This will protect the body from excess acid. A diet too rich in acid-forming foods such as meat, confectionery, alcohol, coffee, and tea creates a great deal of work for the liver and kidneys.

* Choose organically grown produce for preference. The smaller the burden of harmful substances you eat in your food, the more efficiently the liver can do its work, and the fewer such substances can build up in your system. If you wish to avoid genetically modified (GM) foods, read any labels with care and select certified organic produce, as this is not produced from GM ingredients.

* Choose fresh vegetables when you can. If this is not possible, choose frozen. Vegetables for freezing are freshly picked, so offer the best chance of preserving valuable nutrients.

* For those who wish to use them, there are several preparations to assist simple, speedy detoxification and ridding the body of excess fluid; health food stores and pharmacies stock these. For example, artichokes can be found in tablet form. Juices available through these outlets are bean, nettle, watercress, pumpkin, dandelion, parsley, black radish, and other plants with healthgiving properties. Delicious, healthy cocktails can be mixed using some of these, together with fresh fruit and vegetable juices. Of course, this is in addition to eating fresh foods.

* An optional first step to a lasting sense of wellbeing is to observe a 1-2 day fast, during which you should drink only water and juices. People who are underweight, pregnant or unwell should not, however, undertake a fast.

Health-promoting
Food constituents that assist health
foods

FRUIT AND VEGETABLES

ARTICHOKES: Globe artichokes contain cynarin, which stimulates the liver and gallbladder, promotes the flow of blood through them, cleanses them, and also promotes the digestion of fats. Artichokes rid the body of excess fluid and lower the cholesterol level

ASPARAGUS: Aspartic acid is strongly diuretic, stimulates the kidneys, and has a positive effect on the body's metabolism. Potassium rids the body of excess fluid

CHICORY: The bitter constituent intybin has a positive effect on the liver and gallbladder, and on the stomach and intestines. It stimulates digestion and metabolism, cleanses the system and helps rid the body of excess fluid, and promotes blood formation

FENNEL: The volatile oils stimulate liver and kidney activity, and promote digestion

KOHLRABI: Stimulates the flow of bile; also the kidneys. Promotes blood formation.

LEEKS: Promote digestion. The fibre and sticky mucilage from the plant cleanse the intestine; mustard oils stimulate the liver, gallbladder, and kidneys. Along with potassium, they help rid the body of excess fluid

PINEAPPLE: Contains the enzyme bromelin, which promotes metabolism and helps rid the body of excess fluid

POTATOES: Help rid the body of excess fluid

RADISHES: Volatile oils stimulate digestion and the formation of bile; unblock biliary flow; diuretic

SCORZONERA: Diuretic; appetite and digestion-promoting

HERBS AND SPICES

BURNET SAXIFRAGE: Diuretic

DILL: Stimulates urine flow

GARDEN CRESS: Purifies the blood; diuretic; stimulates the metabolism

GINGER: Has volatile oils, hot and bitter constituents. Stimulates the circulation; promotes appetite and digestion

HORSERADISH: Diuretic; stimulates stomach, gallbladder, kidneys, and intestines

JUNIPER: Purifies the blood; diuretic

LOVAGE: Cleansing and purifying; stimulates the flow of bile and secretion of stomach digestive juices; promotes kidney activity

NASTURTIUM: Stimulates the formation of red blood cells, purifies the blood, encourages blood formation and the transport of oxygen around the body

NETTLE: Purifies the blood; increases urine flow. Contains an excess of alkali, so good for de-acidification

PURSLANE: Purifies the blood; diuretic

RAMSONS: Purify the blood; fortifying. Also called broad-leaved garlic

ROCKET, RUCOLA: Regenerates the mucous lining of the gut; contains aspartic acid (diuretic)

TARRAGON: Diuretic; stimulates the metabolism; cleanses kidneys and gallbladder

TURMERIC: Fortifies the liver and gallbladder; purifies the blood; increases production of bile

Substance	Effect	Important sources
Bitter constituents	strengthen the glands producing digestive juices, stimulate the gallbladder, and promote the digestion of fats	broccoli, artichokes, pulses
Calcium	Combats the heavy metals lead and cadmium, preventing their storage in the body	milk, nuts, broccoli, mangold, green cabbage
Chloride	regulates the acid-alkali balance; detoxification	almost all foods
Fibre	stimulates the activity of the intestines, shortening the time that the food remains in the gut; takes up metabolic and other waste products in the stomach and intestines, so that they can be eliminated	grains, pulses, leaf vegetables of cabbage family, peas, carrots, potatoes, apples, pears, berries
Glutathione	sulphur-containing protein; speeding up of detoxification processes in the body	leaf vegetables of cabbage family, radishes (large and small types), root vegetables
Hot constituents	stimulate digestion	spices such as ginger, chili, pepper, paprika
Iron	promotes blood formation; important for transport of oxygen	peas, beans, spinach, nuts, cabbage, grapes, meat
Mustard oils	have a purifying and antiseptic effect; increase activity of stomach and intestines; strengthen liver, gallbladder, kidneys, and bladder	Vegetables of the brassica family such as cabbage, radishes (all types), root vegetables, and of the allium family (onions, leeks)
Potassium	rids the body of excess fluid and purifies (stimulates kidney activity); strengthens blood vessels and kidneys	potatoes, cabbage, brown rice, fruit, grains
Secondary plant substances	protect against free radicals, which are involved in the build-up of impurities in the body; help the cleansing process; can be diuretic	fruit and vegetables
Selenium	binds heavy metals and enables their elimination from the body; stimulates the liver; important for inactivating radicals	almost all types of fruit and vegetables, red cabbage, grains, nuts, pulses, meat
Volatile oil	stimulate the metabolism, and so help to remove harmful substances; stimulate appetite and digestion; cleanse mucous membranes; strengthen the stomach, liver, gallbladder, and intestines	many plants, especially herbs and spices; also fennel, carrots,
Zinc	an aid against stress; decreases the burden on the liver	fish, meat, cheese, grains

Seven-day

Detox with a feast of vitamins

powerfood plan

FITNESS, HEALTH, AND BEAUTY

Would you like to lavish a little more attention on your body and health? To banish that weary feeling—not just in spring—and perk up your metabolism? Cleanse your system, and give your body a detox cure! Over seven days, you can enjoy preparing and eating the recipes given for this one-week powerfood plan. You will reap the benefit in no time, and start feeling and looking healthier.

THE ONE-WEEK DETOX PLAN

If you wish, you can of course use the recipes in this book in whatever order you choose. For those who prefer a ready-made plan, the page opposite provides this. It offers suggestions for the midday and evening meal for each day of the week. These recipes can be interchanged as wished. The best start to the day is a breakfast of rye or wholegrain black bread (such as pumpernickel) or muesli with a flaked wholegrain or shredded cereal base, eaten with fruit and quark or yoghurt. Snacks should consist of raw fruit and vegetables. Use the tables on pages 6 and 7

to select the varieties that help cleanse the body. A carton of yoghurt or cultured milk can also be recommended. For best results, it is important to drink as much as possible during the week of the powerfood plan.

AT WORK ALL DAY?

If you cannot cook two meals a day, or have no wish to, choose one of the recipes to prepare for the evening meal. You can simply take fresh fruit, vegetables, and yoghurt for midday. Again, the tables on pages 6 and 7 will help you choose.

PLAN FOR THE WEEK

Monday

* Breakfast of muesli with fresh fruit, or wholegrain black bread. To drink: buttermilk
* Harlequin vegetable salad; wholewheat baguette
* Asparagus and shrimp risotto * Fresh pineapple

Tuesday

* Breakfast of rye or wholegrain black bread. To drink: a glass of cultured milk
* Salad of chicory and cress * Quick potato curry
* Hearty celeriac and rice pancakes * Fresh fruit

Wednesday

* Breakfast of muesli with fresh fruit, or wholegrain black bread. To drink: buttermilk
* Creamy watercress soup * Herb omelette with asparagus
* Bavette with artichoke sauce * Fresh pineapple

Thursday

* Breakfast of rye or wholegrain black bread. To drink: a glass of cultured milk
* Green corn burgers with salad * Fresh fruit
* Rocket and apple salad, served with fried fillet of chicken

Friday

* Breakfast of muesli with fresh fruit, or wholegrain black bread. To drink: buttermilk
* Fruit and asparagus salad with strawberries and melon; wholewheat baguette
* Salmon with sorrel sauce; new potatoes * Fresh pineapple

Saturday

* Breakfast of rye or wholegrain black bread. To drink: a glass of cultured milk
* Vegetable and yoghurt bake
* Julienne courgettes with red pepper; wholegrain black bread * Potato cream soup with rocket

Sunday

* Breakfast of fresh fruit salad, wholewheat rolls, lean cold meats, one egg
* Chervil in aspic with mustard sauce * Stuffed artichokes
* Asparagus salad with ham; baguette * Fresh pineapple

Asparagus

pine kernels add

salad with

a delicate "bite"

ham

Serves 2: • 400g (14oz) white asparagus • salt • sugar • 1 tsp butter • 1 1/2 tbsp cider vinegar • white pepper • 3 tbsp oil • 4 slices of Parma ham • 2 tbsp pine kernels • fresh basil

Wash, peel and trim the asparagus. Cook the asparagus by steaming it, in an asparagus steamer if available. Bring a small quantity of water to the boil in the outer pot with a little salt and sugar, and the butter. Place the asparagus in the inner steamer, and lower it into the pot with the boiling water. Cover securely and steam for 15-20 minutes, until just tender, still slightly firm.

Mix together the cider vinegar, salt and pepper, then thoroughly beat in the oil. Drain the asparagus well, and cut into chunks. Turn the asparagus in the dressing. Arrange on plates with the Parma ham. Toast the pine kernels, and scatter them over the asparagus, adding a few fresh basil leaves.

PER PORTION: 358 kcal • 17 g protein • 32 g fat • 7 g carbohydrate

Asparagus salad with watercress

wild herbs add a refined touch

Serves 2:
400g (14oz) green asparagus
Salt
1/2 tsp sugar
1 tsp butter
1/2 bunch of watercress
1-2 tbsp walnuts
1-2 tbsp chopped wild herbs
1 tbsp cider vinegar
White pepper
1 tbsp walnut oil
2 tbsp olive or sunflower oil

Wash the asparagus, clean it and peel the lower third of the stems. Cook the asparagus by steaming it, in an asparagus steamer if available. Bring a small quantity of water to the boil in the outer pot with a little salt, the sugar, and butter. Place the asparagus in the inner steamer, and lower it into the pot with the boiling water. Cover securely and steam for 5-8 minutes, until just tender, still slightly firm. Drain well and cut into chunks.

Wash the watercress and shake dry. Sort it, removing any coarse stems. Roughly chop the walnuts.

To make the dressing, mix the herbs with the vinegar and a little salt and pepper. Thoroughly beat the two oils into the mixture. Season.

Turn the asparagus and watercress in the dressing. Arrange on plates and sprinkle with walnuts to serve.

Watercress

This peppery flavoured salad vegetable is full of good and healthy things. Just 100g (4oz) supplies the entire daily requirement of vitamin C. It also contains iron, important in blood formation, and calcium. Watercress purifies the blood, stimulates, and encourages the flow of urine, making it an ideal ingredient in a detox plan.

Per Portion:

251 kcal

6 g protein

22 g fat

7 g carbohydrate

power

Dandelion salad

a stylish springtime salad

with goat's cheese

Preheat the oven to 220°C (425°F). Peel and chop the onion and garlic. Whisk together with the vinegar, salt and pepper, then thoroughly beat in the oil using a balloon whisk.

Wash and sort the dandelion leaves. Shake thoroughly dry and tear into pieces as wished. Turn the leaves in the dressing and arrange on plates. Wash the cherry tomatoes, halve or quarter them, and add to the salad.

Cut the goat's cheese into four rounds and lay these on top of the slices of bread. Place in an ovenproof dish and bake on the middle shelf of the oven until the cheese is hot but not yet melted. Add the slices to the salad, and serve immediately.

Serves 2:

1 small onion

1 small clove of garlic

1-2 tbsp wine vinegar

salt

white pepper

3 tbsp safflower oil

100g (3½ oz) young dandelion leaves

60g (2oz) small cherry tomatoes

1 small round goat's cheese (60g, or 2oz)

4 slices from a baguette loaf

Dandelion

Dandelion contains substances that stimulate the appetite and the digestion. Kidney activity is enhanced by dandelion, which therefore has a diuretic effect. A bitter constituent, choline, acts on liver function, and encourages the flow of bile. Dandelion is therefore popular as a medicinal plant for treating gallbladder, liver, and kidney problems.

PER PORTION:

339 kcal

11 g protein

19 g fat

9 g carbohydrate

power

Fennel and
with fried fillet of rabbit
grapefruit salad

Segment the grapefruit, removing the inner skin and collecting the juice as it drips. Wash the fennel, clean it, and slice the bulb very finely. Chop the green fennel fronds and set aside.

Serves 2:
1 pink grapefruit
1 bulb of fennel
1 shallot
Salt
Black pepper
1 tbsp cider vinegar
3 tbsp oil
1 fillet of rabbit
3 juniper berries
1 small handful of rocket

Peel and chop the shallot finely. Whisk it together with the fennel fronds, salt, pepper, and vinegar in a bowl. Use a balloon whisk to beat in 2 tbsp of the oil, followed by the reserved grapefruit juice. Turn the fennel and grapefruit segments in the dressing.

Rinse the rabbit with cold water and pat dry. Crush the juniper berries using a pestle and mortar, or chop with a large knife. Rub the rabbit meat with the crushed juniper berries, salt, and pepper. Heat the remaining oil in a large frying pan. Brown the meat on all sides, then reduce the heat to medium, and continue to fry for about 5 minutes, until done.

Wash the rocket, shake dry, and sort. Arrange on plates with the fennel and grapefruit salad. Cut the rabbit fillet into thin slices and add to the salad.

PER PORTION: 308 kcal • 24 g protein • 20 g fat • 8 g carbohydrate

Purslane salad
apple dressing lends a touch of sweetness
with beans

Serves 2:

70g (2 1/2 oz) green beans

Salt

1 stalk of summer savory

60g (2oz) small button mushrooms

5 radishes

60-70g (2-2 1/2 oz) purslane

1 shallot

1 small clove of garlic

Black pepper

1 tbsp cider vinegar

2 tsp apple juice (cloudy or home-made)

2 tbsp oil

Rinse and clean the beans, halve if necessary, and place in a small quantity of boiling, salted water in a saucepan with the savory. Cover and steam for 10-15 minutes as necessary.

Meanwhile rinse the mushrooms, or clean with a damp cloth. Slice them finely. Rinse and clean the radishes and cut into thin slices. Wash the purslane, shake dry, sort and clean it.

To make the dressing, peel and chop the shallot and the garlic. Stir together with the salt, pepper, cider vinegar, and apple juice. Whisk in the oil thoroughly with a balloon whisk. Adjust seasoning.

Drain the beans well and turn them in the dressing with the mushrooms, radishes, and purslane.

Purslane

This salad vegetable has green, fleshy leaves which are rich in potassium and iron. Purslane helps flush out the system, and assists blood formation. It also contains healthy omega-3 fatty acids.

PER PORTION:

123 kcal

3 g protein

8 g fat

10 g carbohydrate

Parsnip and carrot rawfood delight

a winter health boost

Toast the walnuts in a dry frying pan. Remove from the heat. Chop about 3 tbsp of the walnuts coarsely and reserve.

Grind the remaining walnuts finely, and mix them with the cream, milk, oil, and vinegar, stirring until smooth. Season with a little coriander, salt, and pepper. Select a little of the green top of the parsnips, wash and shake dry, and chop finely. Stir into the sauce.

Rinse and clean the parsnip and carrot. Slice them thinly or grate them. Arrange the vegetables on plates with the sauce, scatter with the reserved chopped walnuts, and serve immediately.

Serves 2:

30g (1oz) walnuts
4 tbsp single cream
4 tbsp milk
2 tsp safflower oil
1 tbsp cider vinegar
Ground coriander
Salt
Black pepper
150g (5oz) parsnips (with tops)
1 small carrot

Parsnip

This is a typical winter vegetable, and a good source of carbohydrate energy in the cold season of the year. The constituents in parsnip make encouraging reading: just 200g (7oz) contains one third of the daily requirement of vitamin C. In addition, parsnip stimulates the appetite and promotes the flow of urine.

PER PORTION:

223 kcal

6 g protein

17 g fat

10 g carbohydrate

power

Asparagus and
avocado salad
with crisp croutons

Cut away the crusts from the bread. Cut the bread into small dice. Heat the butter in a small saucepan until foaming. Fry the diced bread on all sides in the butter. Cool.

Wash and clean the spring onion and dice finely. Stir together with the apple juice, vinegar, salt, and pepper. Thoroughly beat in the two oils. Rinse and clean the asparagus, and peel it carefully. Cut it diagonally into thin slices and immediately turn the asparagus slices in the dressing.

Wash the tomatoes, cut into wedges, and remove the tough portion next to the stalk. Peel the avocado, cut it in half, and remove the stone. Cut each half crosswise into slices. Sprinkle the slices with lemon juice. Arrange the tomato wedges, slices of avocado, and asparagus salad on plates, sprinkling the tomatoes and avocado with some of the dressing. Scatter with the croutons.

Wash the lemon thyme and shake dry. Strip the leaves from the stems and scatter over the salad. Serve immediately.

Serves 2:

1 slice of wholemeal bread
1 tsp butter
1 tender spring onion
2 tsp apple juice (cloudy)
1 tbsp cider vinegar
Salt, white pepper
1 tbsp olive or sunflower oil
1 tbsp walnut oil
250g (9oz) white asparagus
2 small firm tomatoes
1 small avocado
1-2 tbsp lemon juice
1-2 sprigs of lemon thyme

PER PORTION: 243 kcal • 4 g protein • 18 g fat • 17 g carbohydrate

Light
with yoghurt dressing and pecan nuts
Waldorf salad

Serves 2: • 1 small fresh egg yolk • 2 tsp lemon juice • 2-3 tbsp oil • 50g (1¾ oz) whole yoghurt • salt • black pepper • 2 sticks of celery • 25g (1oz) pecan nuts • 1-2 sharp flavoured apples

Stir together the egg yolk and lemon juice, and whisk in the oil drop by drop. Stir in the yoghurt. Season with salt and pepper. Rinse and clean the celery. Reserve the leaves, and slice the stalks. Chop the nuts coarsely. Wash the apples, and cut them into 1-2cm (½-¾in) dice, removing the cores. Turn all the ingredients in the dressing, check seasoning, and serve, garnished with celery leaves.

PER PORTION: 325 kcal • 5 g protein • 26 g fat • 20 g carbohydrate

Julienne courgettes
vitamins a-plenty in a crunchy treat
with red pepper

Serves 2: • 1 red pepper • salt • black pepper • Tabasco • 1 shallot • 1 small clove of garlic • 1 tbsp cider vinegar • 2 tbsp olive oil • 125g (4oz) courgettes (zucchini)

Rinse and clean the red pepper. Cut into four, and dice one piece finely. Puree and sieve the rest. Season the puree with salt, pepper, and a few drops of Tabasco, and divide between plates. Peel and chop the shallot and the garlic, stir into the vinegar, salt, and pepper, then beat in the oil. Wash and clean the courgettes and cut into fine strips. Turn the strips in the dressing, then arrange on top of the red pepper sauce. Scatter with the diced red pepper.

PER PORTION: 101 kcal • 2 g protein • 8 g fat • 5 g carbohydrate

Rocket salad with
a cleansing salad with a taste of Italy
two cheeses

Brown the pine kernels in a dry frying pan until golden. Set aside. Clean and sort the rocket, wash it, and shake it dry. Tear into small pieces if necessary. Peel the carrot and grate it coarsely. Cut the Fontina cheese into strips. Grate the Parmesan using a suitable grater (a vegetable grater will do).
To make the dressing, peel the shallots and dice very finely. Whisk together with the balsamic vinegar, salt, and pepper. Then beat in the oil thoroughly. Adjust the seasoning.
Turn the rocket, grated carrot and Fontina cheese in the dressing. Scatter with the pine kernels and grated Parmesan.

Serves 2:
2 tbsp pine kernels
75g (2 1/2 oz) rocket (rucola)
1 small carrot
50g (1 3/4 oz) Fontina cheese
20g (3/4 oz) piece of Parmesan cheese
For the dressing:
2 small shallots
1 1/2 tbsp balsamic vinegar
Salt
Black pepper
4 tbsp olive oil

Rocket

Also called roquette or rucola, this well-loved salad vegetable is a relative of the cabbage and of mustard. Like them, it contains volatile oils and organic acids, whose effect is stimulating and awakens the appetite. Rocket is also rich in vitamin C. It rids the body of excess fluid and should certainly feature on the menu in any detox plan.

PER PORTION:

346 kcal

13 g protein

32 g fat

6 g carbohydrate

Harlequin
with herbs and pumpkin seeds
vegetable salad

Serves 2:
1 small red pepper
1 small kohlrabi
1/2 bunch of radishes
125g (4oz) cucumber
1 small onion
1 small clove of garlic
2 tbsp pumpkin seeds
4 stalks of flat-leaved parsley
1 handful of fresh chervil
4 stalks of dill
1 stalk of tarragon
2 tbsp cider vinegar
Salt
Black pepper
2 tbsp safflower oil
1 tbsp pumpkin seed oil

Cut the red pepper in half, trim away the stalk area and inner ribs, and remove the seeds. Wash it. Peel the kohlrabi, and clean and wash the radishes, reserving a little of the green tops of both. Wash or peel the cucumber.

 Cut the red pepper, kohlrabi, and cucumber into approximately 1cm (1/2in) dice. Slice the radishes thinly. Mix the vegetables in a bowl.

 Peel and finely chop the onion and garlic. Put them into a salad bowl. Chop the pumpkin seeds and add to the mixture in the salad bowl. Wash the herbs, along with the pieces of kohlrabi and radish top. Shake dry and chop. Add to the mixture in the salad bowl.

 Stir in the vinegar, and season generously with salt and pepper. Beat in the two oils. Adjust the seasoning, then turn the vegetables in the dressing. Leave to stand for 30 minutes to absorb flavours.

PER PORTION: 219 kcal • 7 g protein • 18 g fat • 9 g carbohydrate

Fruit and

with strawberries and melon

asparagus salad

Wash the asparagus, clean it and carefully peel the lower third. Cook the
asparagus by steaming it, in an asparagus steamer if available. In the

Serves 2:
300g (10oz) green asparagus
1 tsp butter
Salt
Sugar
1/4 of a cantaloupe melon
75g (21/2 oz) strawberries
1 tbsp cider vinegar
1 tsp clear honey
White pepper
3 tbsp oil

outer pot, bring to the boil a small quantity of water
containing the butter, and a little salt and sugar.
Place the asparagus in the inner steamer and lower
into the pot with the boiling water. Cover securely
and steam for 10-15 minutes, until just tender, but
still firm.

Meanwhile remove the seeds and fibrous parts from
the middle of the melon. Use a melon ball cutter to
scoop out the flesh. Wash and drain the strawberries,
trim them and halve or quarter them.

In a salad bowl, whisk together the cider vinegar with the honey and a
little salt and pepper. Thoroughly beat in the oil, using a balloon whisk.
Drain the asparagus thoroughly, and cut into chunks about 3cm (1 1/4in)
long. Turn the asparagus in the dressing, together with the other
ingredients.

power

PER PORTION: 167 kcal • 3 g protein • 13 g fat • 9 g carbohydrate

Sauerkraut salad

cleansing and rich in vitamins

with cress

Thoroughly whisk together the cider vinegar, apple juice, and oil. Season with salt, pepper, and curry powder. With a knife, cut the sauerkraut into small pieces. Turn it in the dressing.

Peel the pineapple with care, cut out the tough middle of the fruit, and dice the flesh. Cut the ham into dice or strips.

Rinse the cress under cold water and shake dry. Use kitchen scissors to cut off the cress required, and mix it with the pineapple, ham, and sauerkraut.

Season the salad generously, and arrange for serving with the nasturtium leaves and flowers.

Serves 2:

2 tsp cider vinegar

1 tbsp apple juice (cloudy)

2 tbsp oil

Salt

Black pepper

¼ tsp curry powder

150g (5oz) sauerkraut

¼ of a pineapple

50g (scant 2oz) boiled ham

½ a box of cress

1 small handful of nasturtium leaves and flowers

Sauerkraut

This contains lactic acid and fibre to stimulate the digestion. The lactic acid also has a cleansing effect. Fresh, raw sauerkraut is the most beneficial to the intestinal flora and digestion, and to health in general. It contains up to 60 per cent more vitamins than canned sauerkraut.

PER PORTION:

203 kcal

6 g protein

12 g fat

19 g carbohydrate

Rocket and
a light, refreshing and crisp salad
apple salad

Brown the pine kernels lightly in a frying pan without fat. Set aside for the topping.

Wash the apple thoroughly, rub it clean, quarter and core it. Dice the fruit and sprinkle it immediately with lemon juice.

Clean and sort the rocket, wash it and shake it thoroughly dry. Tear into conveniently sized pieces if necessary.

To make the dressing, whisk together the apple juice, red wine vinegar, salt, and pepper in a bowl. Then thoroughly beat in the two oils, using a balloon whisk. Adjust the seasoning. Turn the rocket and diced apple in the dressing. Arrange the salad on plates and scatter the pine kernels on top. Grate the Parmesan over the salad before serving.

Serves 2:
2 tbsp pine kernels
1 small red-skinned apple
1 tbsp lemon juice
about 75g (2 1/2 oz) rocket (rucola)
20g (3/4 oz) piece of Parmesan cheese
For the dressing:
1 tbsp apple juice (cloudy or home-made)
1 1/2 tbsp red wine vinegar
salt
black pepper
1 1/2 tbsp olive oil
1 1/2 tbsp pine kernel oil

Alternatives to pine kernel oil

If pine kernel oil does not agree with you, or you cannot obtain it, other nuts and oils can be used instead. Use walnuts and walnut oil, hazelnuts and hazelnut oil, or almonds and almond oil. For a less intense flavour, "dilute" the nut oil with a neutral one.

PER PORTION:

245 kcal

5 g protein

20 g fat

15 g carbohydrate

Herb salad with
with a velvety Parmesan dressing
dry-cured beef

Serves 2:
75g (2 1/2oz) mixed wild and
cultivated herbs
40g (1 1/2oz) dry-cured beef
(Swiss Bundnerfleisch if
available)
1 fresh egg
1 1/2 tbsp oil
3 tbsp dry white wine
1 1/2 tbsp cider vinegar
50g (scant 2oz) grated
Parmesan cheese
3 tbsp wholemilk yoghurt
Salt
Black pepper

Wash the herbs thoroughly and shake dry. Pick them over, and remove the tough stalks. Cut the dry-cured beef into strips and mix with the herbs.

Whisk the egg in a bowl with the oil, wine, and vinegar, then place the bowl over a saucepan of hot water on a medium heat, stirring and whisking constantly to create a light, creamy sauce.

Remove the bowl from the pan of hot water, stir the Parmesan into the sauce, and let it melt. Cool a little, then stir in the yoghurt, and season the sauce with salt and pepper. Arrange the herb mixture on plates, sprinkle the dressing over it, and serve the salad immediately.

Herbs

Wild or cultivated, all herbs are full of healthgiving properties. Fragrant and low in calories, they stimulate the appetite and digestion, and help cleanse the system. You might try dandelion, watercress, sorrel, basil, flat-leaved parsley, and chervil, or use dandelion or rocket alone.

PER PORTION:

265 kcal

20 g protein

18 g fat

1 g carbohydrate

power

Radish and

raw foods with a touch of elegance

kohlrabi carpaccio

Serves 2 • 1/2 bunch of radishes • 2 small kohlrabi • 1 tbsp balsamic vinegar • 1 tbsp apple juice (cloudy or home-made) • 1/4 tsp mustard • salt • black pepper • 1 1/2 tbsp olive oil • 2 tsp pumpkin seed oil • 1 tbsp pumpkin seeds

Wash and clean the radishes and kohlrabi. Peel the kohlrabi. Slice both sets of vegetables thinly. Chop a little of the green tops from the radishes and the kohlrabi, and mix it with the balsamic vinegar, apple juice, mustard, salt, and pepper. Beat in the two oils. Arrange overlapping slices of kohlrabi in a circle around each plate, and arrange the radish inside the ring, also in overlapping slices. Sprinkle on the dressing, and scatter with the pumpkin seeds. **PER PORTION:** 154 kcal • 3 g protein • 12 g fat • 11 g carbohydrate

Salad of chicory

a vitamin boost for chilly days

and cress

Serves 2: • 2 small oranges • 75g (2 1/2 oz) wholemilk yoghurt • salt • white pepper • ground coriander • 2 tbsp grapeseed oil • 1-2 tbsp tomato ketchup • 250g (8oz) chicory • 1/2 box of cress

Peel and segment the oranges, collecting the juice that drips. Mix the juice with the yoghurt, salt, pepper, coriander, grapeseed oil, and tomato ketchup. Wash and clean the chicory, and cut in pieces. Rinse the cress under cold water, and cut off the amount required. Arrange the orange and chicory on plates, sprinkle with dressing and scatter with cress.

PER PORTION: 146 kcal • 4 g protein • 6 g fat • 18 g carbohydrate

Creamy watercress soup

cleansing and tempting

Wash the watercress, and remove any very tough stems. Set aside a few leaves for garnish. Peel and finely dice the onion. Melt 1/2 tbsp butter in a saucepan, and fry the onion in it until transparent. Add the watercress and sweat briefly. Pour on the vegetable stock, and simmer for a few minutes on a low heat.

Purée the soup in a blender, and return it to the saucepan. Stir in the cream, and bring the soup back to boiling point.

Stir a little soup into the egg yolk in a cup until smooth. Add it to the soup, and stir. Do not allow the soup to boil at this stage. Season the soup with salt and a few drops of lemon juice.

Melt the remaining butter in a frying pan. Cut the bread into dice, and fry them in the butter until crisp. Scatter over the soup before serving, and garnish with watercress leaves.

Serves 2:
1/2-1 bunch of watercress
1 small onion
1 tbsp butter
250ml (8fl oz) vegetable stock
100g (31/2 fl oz) single cream
1 egg yolk
salt
lemon juice
1-2 slices wholemeal bread<

power

PER PORTION: 364 kcal • 6 g protein • 23 g fat • 28 g carbohydrate

Potato cream soup

topped with tender almonds

with rocket

Peel, wash and dice the potatoes. Peel and dice the onion. Melt the butter in a saucepan, and fry the onion in it until translucent. Add the diced

Serves 2:	potato and the stock, cover, and simmer for 10-15
300g (10oz) floury potatoes	minutes on a low heat.
1 small onion	
2 tsp butter	Meanwhile, brown the almonds lightly in a dry
400ml (14 fl oz) vegetable stock	frying pan without fat until golden. Remove from the
2 tbsp flaked almonds	heat. Wash the rocket and sort it. Remove the tough
1 small handful of rocket (rucola)	stems and cut the rest into strips.
Salt	Purée the potato soup in a blender. Return it to the
White pepper	saucepan, and bring back to boiling point. Season
70g (2½ fl oz) whipping cream	with salt and pepper. Add the strips of rocket to the soup.

Whip the cream stiffly, and fold it into the soup. Scatter with the almonds before serving.

A soup with a plus

The potassium-rich potatoes and the aspartic acid in rocket, with its diuretic properties, both play a part in cleansing. The extra liquid from the soup is a bonus: it flushes out the kidneys.

PER PORTION:

299 Kcal

5 g protein

19g fat

26g carbohydrate

power

Lentil soup
bacon adds savoury appeal
with cream

Put the lentils and vegetable stock into a large saucepan, and bring to the boil. Reduce the heat to low, and simmer, covered, for about 40 minutes. Cut the bacon into thin strips. Wash and clean the spring onions, and cut them diagonally into dainty rings. Take a few lentils from the soup and set aside. Purée the rest in a blender, and return to the saucepan. Stir in the cream, and return the reserved lentils to the soup. Bring it back to boiling point. Season with salt, pepper, and mustard, aiming for a flavoursome soup. Fry the bacon in a nonstick frying pan until crisp. Add the spring onions, and turn them briefly in the bacon fat, without frying. Season with pepper. Pour the soup into bowls, sprinkle the bacon and spring onions on top, and serve immediately.

Serves 2:

75g (2 1/2 oz) lentils

400ml (14 fl oz) vegetable stock

30g (1oz) bacon

1/2 bunch of spring onions

70ml (2 1/2 fl oz) single cream

Salt

Black pepper

1/2 tsp mild mustard

Lentils and mustard

Lentils are rich in fibre. This stimulates and protects the intestines. It prevents impurities from collecting. Mustard contains the glycoside sinigrin and the enzyme myrosin. Moisture causes them to react with each other, releasing volatile oil of mustard. This has a cleansing, antiseptic effect.

PER PORTION:

355 Kcal

14 g protein

21 g fat

25 g carbohydrate

power

Salmon and

light luxury

asparagus soup

Serves 2:

300g (10½ oz) white asparagus

Salt

Sugar

1½ tbsp butter

100g (3½ oz) fresh peas in the pod (about 50g [scant 2oz] when shelled)

100g (3½ oz) salmon fillet

1 tbsp lemon juice

1 tbsp flour

50g (scant 2oz) crème fraîche

Wash and clean the asparagus. Peel it carefully, reserving the trimmings. Cut off the tips, cover, and set aside. Cut up the stems and put into a saucepan with 125ml (4fl oz) water, a pinch each of salt and sugar, and 1/2 tsp butter. Bring to the boil, cover, and cook for 15 minutes. Then purée the cooked asparagus pieces with their cooking liquid.

Meanwhile, place the asparagus peel into a saucepan with the reserved trimmings. Add 250ml (8fl oz) water, a pinch each of salt and sugar, and 1/2 tsp butter. Cover and simmer for 15 minutes. Strain the cooking liquid.

Meanwhile, shell the peas. Wash the salmon and cut it into dice. Sprinkle it with lemon juice.

Melt the remaining butter in a saucepan. Stir in the flour, and cook until the mixture becomes golden. Pour on the strained cooking liquid from the asparagus trimmings, stir in; add the asparagus purée and crème fraîche. Place the asparagus tips, peas, and salmon in the soup, and cook through for a further 2-3 minutes. Season the soup and serve immediately.

PER PORTION: 291 kcal • 15 g protein • 21 g fat• 10 g carbohydrate

Chilled cucumber

refreshment for hot summer days

soup

Serves 2: • 250g (9oz) cucumber • 150g (5oz) wholemilk yoghurt • 75g (2¹/₂ oz) crème fraîche • 100ml (3¹/₂ fl oz) cultured milk • 1 clove of garlic • salt • black pepper • 1 tomato • 2 stalks of dill

Peel the cucumber and grate it coarsely. Stir it into the yoghurt, crème fraîche, and cultured milk. Peel the garlic and crush into the soup mixture. Season with salt and pepper. Cover and chill for 2 hours. Wash the tomato and dill. Dice the tomato finely. Select the delicate ends of the dill and pull away from the coarser stalk. Scatter dill and tomato on to the soup.

PER PORTION: 240 kcal • 6 g protein• 20 g fat • 9 g carbohydrate

Sumptuous

with piquant rocket-leaf cream garnish

sauerkraut soup

Serves 2: • 1 small onion • 1 small floury potato • 1 tbsp butter • 150g (5oz) sauerkraut • 400ml (14fl oz) vegetable stock • 50g (scant 2oz) rocket (rucola)• 50g (scant 2oz) crème fraîche • salt • black pepper

Peel and dice the onion and the potato. Sweat these in the butter in a saucepan. Add the sauerkraut and the vegetable stock. Cover, and simmer for 10 minutes. Wash and sort the rocket, and purée it with the crème fraîche, using a blender. Season with salt and pepper. Purée the soup, return it to boiling point, and top with the rocket-leaf purée to serve.

PER PORTION: 211 kcal • 3 g protein• 16 g fat • 16 g carbohydrate

Chervil

a soup with a creamy mousse

soup

Peel the onion and potatoes, and dice coarsely. Melt the butter in a saucepan, and sweat the onion and potato dice, stirring constantly. Pour on the stock, cover, and simmer for at least 20 minutes on a low heat.

Rinse and sort the chervil thoroughly, and shake dry. Set aside a little chervil for garnish. Chop the rest, and stir it into the soup.

Purée the soup with a hand blender or other. Stir in the crème fraîche, and reheat the soup to boiling point. Season with salt, pepper, and a little coriander. Whisk again with the hand blender to a frothy consistency, and scatter with chervil before serving.

Serves 2:

1 small onion

125g (4oz) floury potatoes

1 tbsp butter

400ml (14fl oz) chicken or vegetable stock

Plenty of fresh chervil

50g (scant 2oz) crème fraîche

Salt

White pepper

Ground coriander

Chervil

This delicate spring herb stimulates the circulation, cleanses the blood, and encourages the flow of urine and sweat, all of benefit in a detox plan. It also has volatile oils and bitter constituents, which promote digestion by stimulating the secretion of stomach juices.

PER PORTION:

171 Kcal

6g protein

15g fat

14g carbohydrate

Chervil in aspic with
stacks of appeal, but not calories
mustard sauce

Boil the egg for 8 minutes, until cooked hard. Rinse the egg in cold water, and peel it. Wash, sort and dry the chervil. Set aside a few pieces of chervil for garnish, wrapped in a clean, damp cloth in a cool place. Chop the remaining chervil a little finer, and mix it into the stock.

Sprinkle the gelatine over the stock in the saucepan and heat gently, stirring, until the gelatine is fully dissolved.

Mix with the rest of the stock. Season, aiming for a piquant flavour. Pour a little of the stock mixture into two moulds (timbales or cups). Place in the refrigerator to set.

Cut the egg in half crosswise. As soon as the gelatine stock in the moulds has set, place one half of the egg on each, cut side down. Pour the remaining stock over it, and replace in the refrigerator to set.

Mix the quark, milk, and mustard, and season with salt and pepper. Place the moulds momentarily in hot water, to loosen them, then turn them out on to plates. Spoon a little sauce alongside. Garnish with chervil to serve.

Serves 2:

1 egg
7g (1/4oz) powdered gelatine
1 handful of chervil
125ml (4fl oz) vegetable stock
Salt
White pepper
Tabasco
2-3 tbsp quark (curd cheese)
3-4 tbsp milk
1 tsp mild mustard

PER PORTION: 91 kcal • 7 g protein • 5 g fat • 3 g carbohydrate

Light herb
with the sharp taste of radish vinaigrette
mousse

Serves 2:
7g (1/4 oz) powdered gelatine
1 bunch of mixed herbs (e.g. sorrel, parsley, dill, basil, tarragon)
75g (2 1/2 oz) wholemilk yoghurt
Salt
White pepper
70ml (2 1/2 fl oz) whipping cream
5 radishes
2 tsp cider vinegar
2 tbsp oil

Sprinkle the gelatine on to a few tbsp of water in a cup, and warm it by standing the cup in hot water, stirring occasionally, until the gelatine has dissolved.

Wash and pick over the herbs, and shake dry. Set aside some of the herbs for garnish. Chop the rest finely.

Mix the dissolved gelatine with the yoghurt and herbs. Season generously with salt and pepper.

Whip the cream until stiff, and fold it into the herb mixture. Transfer it to a small ring mould or to two cups. Cover, and place in the refrigerator to set.

Just before serving, wash, clean and coarsely grate the radishes. Mix them with the cider vinegar and a little salt and pepper. Thoroughly beat in the oil with a balloon whisk. Adjust seasoning. Place the mould or cups with the mousse momentarily in hot water, to loosen the edges. Turn out the mousse. Garnish with herbs, and arrange with the vinaigrette to serve.

PER PORTION: 215 kcal • 4 g protein • 20 g fat • 3 g carbohydrate

Herb omelette with

succulent and quick to do

asparagus

Serves 2: • 250g (9oz) green asparagus • salt • 1½ tbsp butter • 1 tsp sugar • 4 eggs • 2 tbsp milk • white pepper • 2 tbsp chopped parsley • 1-2 tbsp chervil

Wash and clean the asparagus, and steam it for about 10 minutes over a little boiling, salted water with 1 tsp each of butter and sugar. Whisk together the eggs, milk, salt, pepper, and herbs. Make two omelettes one after the other in a nonstick frying pan with the remaining butter. Drain the asparagus well, wrap in the omelettes, and serve.

PER PORTION: 246 kcal • 17 g protein • 17 g fat • 6 g carbohydrate

Hearty celeriac

with fresh herb yoghurt

and rice pancakes

Serves 2: • 80g (3oz) brown rice • salt • 75g (2½ oz) wholemilk yoghurt • 1 tbsp full fat cream cheese • white pepper • 2 tbsp chopped herbs • 1 tsp apple juice (cloudy or home-made) • 150g (5oz) celeriac • 2 eggs • oil

Cook the rice in 160ml (generous 5fl oz) water until just tender, still firm. Mix the yoghurt, cream cheese, salt, pepper, herbs, and apple juice. Peel and coarsely grate the celeriac. Drain the rice, and mix with the celeriac and the eggs. Season with salt and pepper. Heat a little oil in a frying pan, and spoon out portions of the mixture to fry a succession of small pancakes. Serve with the herb yoghurt.

PER PORTION: 354 kcal • 13 g protein • 18 g fat • 36 g carbohydrate

Artichokes with dips

imaginative food for guests

Place plenty of salted water in a large saucepan with a few lemon slices. Break off the stems of the artichokes with a quick tug. Cut off the top third of the leaves. Place in the water and boil over a medium heat for 40 minutes. The artichokes are cooked when the leaves can be pulled away easily. Boil the egg for 8-10 minutes until cooked hard. Peel and separate the yolk and the white. Pass the yolk through a fine sieve, and mix it with the cider vinegar, salt, and pepper. Beat in the oil gradually. Wash the sorrel, shake dry, and remove the tough stalks. Chop the leaves. Dice the egg white finely. Mix the sorrel, egg white, and sour cream into the sauce. Season, aiming for a piquant taste. Wash, clean and grate the radishes. Stir together the cream cheese and milk, season with salt, pepper, and a little cardamom, then add the grated radishes. Lift the artichokes out of the water and drain them. Serve with the dips.

Serves 2:

Salt

Lemon slices

2 globe artichokes (each about 500g) (18oz)

1 egg

2 tsp cider vinegar

White pepper

3-4 tbsp olive oil

1/2 bunch of sorrel

50ml (scant 2fl oz) sour cream

1/2 bunch of radishes

60g (2oz) full fat cream cheese

4-5 tbsp milk

cardamom

Eating artichokes

Pull away one leaf at a time, holding it in your fingers. Dip the fleshy base of the leaf in one of the dips, and eat it by drawing the leaf base through your teeth to skim off the flesh of the vegetable. When you have pulled away all the leaves, you will find the fibrous "choke" in the middle. This cannot be eaten. Lift it off, and underneath, you will find the delicious, succulent "heart" of the artichoke.

PER PORTION:

381 Kcal

13 g protein

32 g fat

11 g carbohydrate

Green cornmeal burgers

to eat at home or take to the office

with piquant salad

Serves 2:

125ml (4fl oz) vegetable stock

60g green cornmeal (fine ground)

1 small carrot

1 small kohlrabi

1 small egg

1/2-1 bunch of dill

Salt

Black pepper

2-3 tbsp breadcrumbs

3 tbsp oil

1/2 small black radish

1/2 bunch of salad radishes

2 tbsp wholemilk yoghurt

1 tbsp full fat cream cheese

1/8 tsp cumin

Bring the vegetable stock to the boil, and cook the cornmeal on a very low heat for 10 minutes, keeping the saucepan firmly covered. Peel the carrot and kohlrabi, and grate finely. Add the vegetables to the cornmeal, and cook together for another 5 minutes. Transfer to a bowl. Stir in the egg, and allow the mixture to cool a little.

Wash the dill and shake dry. Discard the tough stalks, and chop. Stir into the green cornmeal mixture. Season with salt and pepper. Add enough breadcrumbs to create a mixture that holds together well. Divide and shape into 4 burgers. Heat the oil in a nonstick frying pan, and fry the burgers for 10 minutes on a very low heat, turning occasionally.

Meanwhile, peel the radish and wash the salad radishes. Coarsely grate both. Stir together the grated radishes, yoghurt, and cream cheese. Season with salt, pepper, and cumin. Serve to accompany the burgers.

PER PORTION: 337 kcal • 10 g protein • 18 g fat • 33 g carbohydrate

Vegetable
with ham and herb dip
crunch

To make the dip, cut the ham into very small dice. Wash, dry, and sort the herbs. Pluck them away from the tough stalks. Reserve a few leaves for garnish, and chop the rest. Rinse the lemon in hot water and dry it. Grate the outer rind and squeeze out the juice.

Mix the ham, herbs, lemon zest, some lemon juice, the almonds, and the quark. Season the dip generously with salt and pepper.

Remove the outer leaves of the chicory. Cut the chicory in half, and make a wedge-shaped cut to remove the stalks. Separate into individual leaves. Wash and clean the rest of the vegetables. Cut them into long strips, just wide enough to manage easily. Arrange all the vegetables on a large platter, accompanied by the dip. Garnish with herbs, and serve.

Serves 2:

40g (1½ oz) boiled ham

1 handful of fresh herbs

1/2 an unwaxed lemon

3 tbsp chopped almonds

125g (4oz) quark (curd cheese) (20% fat)

Salt

Black pepper

1 head of chicory

1/2 a small head of celery

1 small courgette (zucchini)

1 carrot

1 small kohlrabi

1 small red pepper

PER PORTION: 229 kcal • 17 g protein • 12 g fat • 12 g carbohydrate

Asparagus and prawn risotto

just as delicious made with small shrimps

Wash the asparagus, peel the lower third, and cut into pieces 3-4cm (1 1/4-1 1/2in) long. Cut off the asparagus tips, cover, and set aside. Wash and clean the spring onions. Cut the green part diagonally into fine rings. Chop the white part small.

Heat the butter and oil gently. Fry the white pieces of onion until transparent. Add the pieces of asparagus stem, followed by the rice. Stir, and pour on the wine. Cook on a low heat, stirring occasionally, until the rice has taken up all the liquid. Then start adding the vegetable stock little by little, allowing each addition to be absorbed.

After 10 minutes, stir in the asparagus tips and the green pieces of spring onion.

Cook the rice until it is done, but still slightly firm, and the mixture remains creamy. Add the prawns, mix, and heat through. Season the risotto with salt and pepper, and sprinkle with Parmesan to serve.

Serves 2:

250g (9oz) green asparagus

1/2 bunch of spring onions

1 tbsp butter

2 tsp olive oil

200g (7oz) risotto rice

150ml (5fl oz) dry white wine

about 400ml (14fl oz) vegetable stock

Salt

White pepper

100g (31/2 oz) peeled cooked prawns or shrimps

30g (1oz) freshly grated Parmesan

power

PER PORTION: 622 kcal • 26 g protein • 12 g fat • 85 g carbohydrate

Stuffed

with a succulent mushroom and ham filling

artichokes

Preheat the oven to 180°C (350°F). Heat plenty of salted water in a large saucepan, and add the lemon juice or vinegar. Break off the stems of the artichokes with a quick tug. Remove the outer leaves, and trim off the tops of any very pointed leaves. Boil the artichokes in the water for 40 minutes on a medium heat. They are cooked when the leaves can be pulled away easily.

Serves 2:

Salt

2 tbsp lemon juice or vinegar

2 large globe artichokes

1 onion

150g (5oz) button mushrooms

1 clove of garlic

2 tbsp olive oil

40g (1 1/2 oz) boiled ham

1-2 stalks each of thyme, rosemary, parsley, basil

2 slices wholemeal bread

60g (2oz) Alpine cheese, grated

Black pepper

Peel the onion and chop finely. Wash, clean, and chop the mushrooms. Peel the garlic. Heat the oil, and fry the onion until translucent. Crush the garlic into the onion, add the mushrooms, and cook on a low heat for 5 minutes. Dice the ham finely. Wash, dry, and chop the herbs. Stir the ham and herbs into the mushroom mixture, and remove from the heat. Lift the artichokes out of the water, and drain thoroughly upside down. Fold open the outer leaves and pull out the soft leaves from the middle. Remove the "choke" with a spoon.

Cut the bread into small dice, add to the mushroom mixture, and stir in the cheese. Season with salt and pepper. Stuff the artichokes with the filling. Place them side by side in an ovenproof dish, and bake in the middle of the oven for 20 minutes.

PER PORTION: 366 kcal • 22 g protein • 21 g fat • 21 g carbohydrate

Salmon with
serve with new potatoes
sorrel sauce

Wash and sort the sorrel. Set aside a few leaves and chop the rest. Peel and finely chop the shallot. Melt 1/2 tbsp butter in a small saucepan, and fry the shallot until translucent. Sprinkle with the flour, and cook briefly. Pour on the stock, stirring. Add the chopped sorrel. Cover, and simmer on a low heat for 5 minutes.

Wash the salmon fillets in cold water, and dry them. Melt the remaining butter in a nonstick frying pan until frothy. Cook the salmon for 3-5 minutes on each side, on a low heat.

Stir crème fraîche into the sorrel sauce, and season with salt, pepper, and a pinch of sugar. Cut the remaining sorrel leaves into fine strips. Arrange the salmon and sauce on plates, and scatter strips of sorrel on top before serving.

Serves 2:
50g (scant 2oz) sorrel
1 shallot
1 tbsp butter
1/2 tbsp flour
200ml (7fl oz) salmon stock
(ready-made if wished)
2 salmon fillets (each 175g/6oz)
2-3 tbsp crème fraîche
Salt
White pepper
Sugar

Sorrel

This salad herb is rich in iron, vitamin C, and bitter constituents. It stimulates the appetite, has a diuretic effect, and promotes blood formation and cleansing. It is beneficial to the liver. However, it should not be eaten in excessive quantities, because the oxalic acid it contains forms insoluble calcium salts, which can lead to kidney stones.

power

PER PORTION:

438 Kcal

36 g protein

35 g fat

5 g carbohydrate

Many-coloured

Asian inspiration with hot spices and vitamins

vegetable curry

Slit open the chili peppers, and remove the seeds. Wash and chop the chilies. Peel and chop the garlic and ginger. Mix all together. Chop the

Serves 2:
1-2 red chili peppers
1 clove of garlic
15g (1/2oz) ginger
50g (scant 2oz) creamed coconut (block)
6 tbsp vegetable stock
2 tbsp soy sauce
1 tbsp curry paste
2 sticks of celery
1 carrot
1/2 bunch of spring onions (green onions)
80g (3oz) broccoli
50g (scant 2oz) beansprouts
1 1/2 tbsp oil
2 sprigs of mint

block of creamed coconut, and heat it in a saucepan with the stock, soy sauce, and curry paste.

Wash and clean the vegetables. Slice the celery, carrot, and spring onions finely. Separate the broccoli into small florets. Rinse the beansprouts well in a colander, and drain thoroughly.

Heat the oil in a wok or frying pan. Fry the chili mixture for 1 minute, stirring. Add the celery, carrot, spring onions, and broccoli, and fry for another 2-3 minutes. Then add the beansprouts, and stir-fry for another 3 minutes.

Pour the coconut sauce into the wok, and cook all the ingredients together for 1-2 minutes. Just before serving, wash and dry the mint, and cut the leaves into thin strips. Sprinkle over the vegetables.

power

PER PORTION: 245 kcal • 5 g protein • 20 g fat • 12 g carbohydrate

Pan-cooked

with broccoli and ewe's milk cheese

red lentils

Serves 2: • 250g (9oz) broccoli • 1 small onion • 1 tbsp olive oil • 100g (3 1/2 oz) red lentils • 250ml (8fl oz) vegetable stock • salt • black pepper • 1 tsp thyme • 100g (3 1/2 oz) ewe's milk cheese

Wash and clean the broccoli, and separate it into florets. Peel the onion. Dice it finely, and fry it in the oil in a broad-based frying pan until transparent. Add the broccoli, lentils, stock, salt, pepper, and thyme. Cook for 6 minutes. Crumble the ewe's milk cheese, and add to the lentils. Cook together for another 1 minute.

PER PORTION: 364 kcal • 25 g protein • 14 g fat • 33 g carbohydrate

Yoghurt and

a meatless meal from the oven

vegetable bake

Serves 2: • 500-600g (1lb-1 1/4lb) mixed vegetables • 3 small eggs • 250g (9oz) wholemilk yoghurt • 25g (1oz) flour • 25g (1oz) chopped almonds • salt • black pepper • 1/2 bunch of parsley • 1/2 box of cress

Preheat the oven to 200°C (400°F). Wash and clean the vegetables, and cut into bite-sized pieces. Boil them for 5 minutes in a small amount of water. Drain well. Crack the eggs, and separate the yolks from the whites. Mix the yoghurt, flour, chopped almonds, salt, pepper, chopped parsley and cress, and egg yolks. Beat the egg whites stiffly, and fold into the mixture. Place the vegetables in a baking dish, and pour the yoghurt mixture over. Bake in the middle of the oven for 20-25 minutes.

PER PORTION: 380 kcal • 22 g protein • 21 g fat • 24 g carbohydrate

Asparagus gratin with
herb cream
topped with cheese and almonds

Preheat the oven to 200°C (400°F). Wash and clean the asparagus, and peel the lower third. Boil a little water in an asparagus steamer or suitable saucepan, and add salt, sugar, and the butter. Place the asparagus in the inner steamer. Cook, covered, for 15 minutes, until just tender, but still firm.

Butter a shallow, ovenproof dish. Wash the tarragon, thyme, and lemon balm, and dry them. Strip the leaves from the stalks, and chop finely. Mix the herbs, sour cream, and eggs. Season with salt and pepper. Drain the asparagus thoroughly, and place it in the buttered baking dish. Pour on the herb cream mixture. Sprinkle with the cheese and almonds, and bake in the middle of the oven for 30 minutes.

Serves 2:
500g (generous 1lb) green asparagus
Salt
Sugar
1 tsp butter
2 sprigs of tarragon
2 sprigs of thyme
2 sprigs of lemon balm
200g (7fl oz) sour cream (24% fat)
2 large or 3 small eggs
White pepper
40g (11/2 oz) grated Emmenthal cheese
2 tbsp flaked almonds
Softened butter for greasing

PER PORTION: 483 kcal • 20 g protein • 41 g fat • 9 g carbohydrate

Bavette with

a cleansing and stylish pasta dish

artichoke sauce

Put plenty of water in a saucepan, and add the lemon juice or vinegar and some salt. The artichoke hearts are needed for this dish. Remove the stems of the artichokes with a sharp tug. Cut off the top half of the leaves. Detach the lower leaves, and peel away around the hearts with a sharp knife. Scrape out the "choke" with a teaspoon. Immediately place the trimmed artichoke hearts into the pan of water containing the lemon juice or vinegar. Bring to the boil, and cook for about 10 minutes until done. Lift out and drain the artichoke hearts, then cut into pieces.

Peel and cut up the onions. Peel the garlic, and cut into strips. Wash the herbs, shake dry, and roughly chop the leaves. Bring a generous quantity of salted water to the boil. Use at least 2 litres (around 4 pints). Cook the pasta in this until just tender. Heat the oil gently. The frying pan should not be too small. Fry the onions and garlic until transparent. Add and heat through the artichoke hearts and herbs, pour on the rose wine, then season with salt and pepper, and simmer gently.

Drain the pasta, add to the other ingredients in the frying pan, and mix. Sprinkle with Parmesan to serve.

Serves 2:
2 tbsp lemon juice or vinegar
Salt
2 large globe artichokes
125g (4oz) red onions
2 small cloves of garlic
2 sprigs each of thyme and marjoram
1 small sprig of rosemary
200g (7oz) bavette or spaghetti
6 tbsp olive oil
6 tbsp rose wine
Black pepper
40g (1½ oz) freshly grated Parmesan

power

PER PORTION: 763 kcal • 27 g protein • 31 g fat • 88 g carbohydrate

Quick potato

a hot curry dish from India

curry

Wash and peel the potatoes, and cut into bite-sized chunks. Heat the oil in a large frying pan. Fry the potatoes on a medium heat for 20 minutes, stirring and turning frequently.

Serves 2:

400g (14oz) potatoes (a variety that stays firm when boiled)

1 tbsp oil

2 small tomatoes

1/2 bunch spring onions (green onions)

1 clove of garlic

15g (1/2 oz) ginger

1/2-1 green chili pepper

1/2 tsp garam masala

1/4 tsp flour

80g (3oz) wholemilk yoghurt

1 tbsp lemon juice

Salt, black pepper

1-2 tsp black sesame seeds

Meanwhile, skin the tomatoes, first pouring boiling water over them to loosen the skin. Dice them. Wash and clean the spring onions. Slice them finely into rings, reserving a little of the green for garnish. Peel the garlic and ginger. Slit open, clean, and wash the chili. Chop all these, and add to the potatoes, together with the spring onions. Fry briefly. Sprinkle on the garam masala, and stir in.

Blend the flour and yoghurt until smooth. Combine with the potatoes, then add the tomatoes. Cook on a low heat for another 10 minutes.

Season the potatoes with the lemon juice, salt, and pepper. Sprinkle with the spring onion rings and sesame seeds, and serve.

PER PORTION: 205 kcal • 6 g protein • 7 g fat • 30 g carbohydrate

Asparagus

a fresh and unusual combination

stir-fry

Serves 2: • 1/2 bunch of spring onions (green onions) • 60g (2oz) shiitake mushrooms • 1 carrot • 400g (14oz) green asparagus • 200g (7oz) boneless chicken breast • 1 tbsp oil • 1 tbsp soy sauce • 5 tbsp white wine • black pepper

Wash, clean, and cut up the spring onions, mushrooms, and carrots. Wash the asparagus, peel the lower third, and cut into pieces. Cube the chicken. Heat the oil in a wok, and stir-fry the asparagus and carrot for 3 minutes. Add the mushrooms and onions, and fry together for 2 minutes. Move the vegetables aside and fry the meat on all sides to seal. Pour on the soy sauce and wine, season with pepper, and fry for 3 minutes.

PER PORTION: 309 kcal • 32 g protein • 6 g fat • 31 g carbohydrate

Tagliatelle with

a quick and delicious dish

asparagus

Serves 2:• 1 onion • 250g (9oz) asparagus • salt • 200g (7oz) green tagliatelle • 1 tbsp butter• 100ml (3 1/2 fl oz) vegetable stock • 100g (3 1/2 oz) full fat cream cheese • white pepper • chervil

Peel and dice the onion finely. Wash, clean, and peel the asparagus. Slice it, leaving the tips whole. Boil the pasta in salted water until just tender and drain. Meanwhile sweat the onions and asparagus in the butter until the onions become translucent. Add the stock, cream cheese, salt, and pepper. Cover and cook for 10 minutes. Sprinkle with chervil and serve with the pasta.

PER PORTION: 551 kcal • 18 g protein • 20 g fat • 77 g carbohydrate

Asparagus and
with red Camargue rice
chicken ragout

Wash, clean, and thoroughly peel the asparagus. Bring 200ml (7fl oz) water to the boil (in an asparagus steamer if available). Add some salt and the sugar. Place the asparagus in the inner steamer, cover with a well-fitting lid, and steam for 10-15 minutes, until just tender, but still firm. Drain, reserving the cooking liquid. Cut into 3cm (1¼ in) pieces.

Serves 2:
500g (generous 1lb) white asparagus
¼ tsp sugar
Salt
150g (generous 5oz) Camargue red rice (alternatively brown rice)
200g (7oz) boneless chicken breast
White pepper
1½ tbsp butter
1 tbsp flour
200ml (7fl oz) chicken stock (may use ready-made stock)
Chervil or parsley

Meanwhile, bring 300ml (10fl oz) water to the boil in a lidded saucepan. Sprinkle in the rice, cover firmly, and cook on a low heat for 30-40 minutes until the rice has swelled. Meanwhile, rinse the chicken in cold water, dry, cut into 2-3cm (about 1in) cubes, and season with pepper.

Melt the butter in a saucepan until it foams. Fry the chicken on all sides until golden, and remove from the pan. Sprinkle the flour into the butter, mix, and cook until golden. Stir in the stock, blending it in well. Pour in the asparagus cooking liquid, and cook on a high heat, stirring, until the mixture acquires a creamy consistency. Wash the chervil or parsley, and chop or tear it into pieces. Stir into the sauce, and add the asparagus and chicken. Return to the boil, season with salt and pepper, and serve with the rice.

PER PORTION: 494 kcal • 34 g protein • 14 g fat • 65 g carbohydrate power

Index to recipes

Detox - foods to cleanse and purify from the within

Abbreviations

tsp = teaspoon
tbsp = tablespoon
kcal = kilocalories

Nutritional analyses in
each recipe refer to the
metric measurements

Most of the ingredients required for the recipes in this book are easily available from supermarkets and health food stores. In case of difficulty, contact the following importers of organic German produce:-
The Organic Food Company, Unit 2, Blacknest Industrial Estate, Blacknest Road, Alton GU34 4PX; (T) 01420 520530 (F) 01420 23985
Windmill Organics, 66 Meadow Close, London SW20 9JD
(T) 0181 395 9749 (F) 0181 286 4732
Fermented Wheat Juice is produced in Germany by Kanne Brottrunk GMBH
(T) 00 49 2592 97400 (F) 00 49 2592 61370
Further information on German food importers is available from The Central Marketing Organisation
(T) 0181 944 0484 (F) 0181 944 0441

First published in the UK by
Gaia Books Ltd., 20 High St
Stroud, GL5 1AZ

Registered at 66 Charlotte St,
London W1P 1LR
Originally published under the title
Entschlacken mit Genuss

© 1999 Gräfe und Unzer Verlag GmbH
Munich. English translation copyright
© 1999 Gaia Books Ltd.
Translated by Elaine Richards in
association with First Edition Translations
Ltd, Cambridge, UK.

Reproduction: MRM Graphics Ltd,
Winslow, UK.
Printed in Singapore by Imago

ISBN 1 85675 150 3
A catalogue record for this book is
available in the British Library

10 9 8 7 6 5 4 3 2

Caution

The techniques and recipes in this book
are to be used at the reader's sole
discretion and risk.
Always consult a doctor if you are in doubt
about a medical condition.

Angelika Ilies

A native of Hamburg, Germany, Angelika
Ilies studied ecotrophology, and launched
her career immediately with a renowned
publishing house in London. Returning to
her home country, she employed her skills
in the service of Germany's biggest food
magazine. Since 1989, she has enjoyed a
successful career as a freelance author and
food journalist.

Photographs: FoodPhotography Eising,
Munich

Susie M. and **Pete Eising** have studios in
Munich and Kennebunkport, Maine, USA.
They studied at the Munich Academy of
Photography, where they established their
own studio for food photography in 1991.

Food styling: **Monika Schuster**

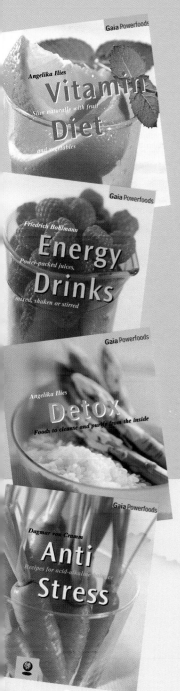

Vitamin Diet

Lose weight naturally with fresh fruit and vegetables
Angelika Ilies
£4.99
ISBN 1 85675 145 7

All the benefits of eating fresh fruit and vegetables plus a natural way to weight loss.

Energy Drinks

Power-packed juices, mixed, shaken or stirred
Friedrich Bohlmann
£4.99
ISBN 1 85675 140 6

Fresh juices packed full of goodness for vitality and health

Detox

Foods to cleanse and purify from within
Angelika Ilies
£4.99
ISBN 1 85675 150 3

Detoxify your body as part of your daily routine by eating nutritional foods that have cleansing properties

Anti Stress

Recipes for Acid-Alkaline Balance
Dagmar von Cramm
£4.99
ISBN 1 85675 155 4

A balanced diet to reduce stress levels, maximise immunity and help you keep fit

For a catalogue of titles please call 01453 752985 or visit our website www.gaiabooks.co.uk

GAIA